THE
100
METHOD

How 100 Minutes a Day for 100 Days Will Change Your Life

THE 100 METHOD™

THE 100 METHOD

How 100 Minutes a Day for 100 Days Will Change Your Life

Copyright © 2026 Kendra Tamika. All rights reserved.

Published by Remember Her Publishing

First Edition

ISBN: 979-8-9955165-6-9
LCCN: 2026911069

theonehundredmethod.com

INTRODUCTION

A Letter to the Reader Who Is Ready

You have been ready for longer than you know. You just needed a method.

This book is for the person who has a goal they haven't yet achieved. Not because they aren't capable. Not because the goal is too big. But because somewhere between the wanting and the doing, something got in the way. Maybe it was life. Maybe it was doubt. Maybe it was a plan that was too complicated, too vague, or too easy to abandon when things got hard.

Whatever it was. It ends here.

The 100 Method is not a motivational book. Motivation is available everywhere, and it has not been enough. What you need is not another reason to want the thing, you already want it. What you need is a clear, simple, repeatable system that works regardless of how you feel on any given day. A method that shows up even when you don't feel like it. A structure that holds you when willpower runs out.

That is what this book gives you.

The Idea Behind the Method

The 100 Method is built on three numbers: 100 minutes, 100 days, and 1 goal.

One hundred minutes of focused effort every single day. Not scattered across ten tasks. Not split between competing priorities. One hundred minutes dedicated entirely to one goal, the one that matters most to you right now.

One hundred days. Long enough to build something real. Short enough that you can see the finish line from the start. Long enough to change who you are. Short enough that every day counts.

One goal. This is perhaps the most radical part of the method. Not a list of goals. Not a vision board full of aspirations. One goal, chosen with intention, pursued with full commitment, protected like the most important thing in your life. Because for the next 100 days, it is.

These three numbers work together to create something that most approaches to goal-setting never achieve: a system that is simple enough to sustain and powerful enough to transform.

"100 minutes. 100 days. 1 goal. Simple by design. Transformative by nature."

What This Book Is, and What It Is Not

This book will not tell you that change is easy. It is not. There will be days in your 100 when you do not want to show up, when the goal feels far away, when the effort seems disproportionate to the progress you can see. This book will not pretend those days don't exist.

What this book will do is give you a framework for those days, a philosophy, a set of practices, and a way of thinking about yourself and your goal that makes showing up possible even when it is hard.

This is a book about becoming. Not just achieving a goal, but becoming the kind of person who achieves it. The kind of person who keeps their word to themselves. The kind of person who builds trust with themselves, one kept promise at a time, until that trust becomes an unshakeable foundation.

By the time you reach the end of this book, and certainly by the time you reach Day 100 — you will not just have made progress on your goal. You will have become someone different. Someone who knows, from lived experience, that they are capable of more than they previously believed.

How to Use This Book

Read this book straight through, beginning to end, before you start your 100 days. Let the ideas settle. Let the framework become familiar. Then return to individual chapters as touchstones when you need them most, when consistency wavers, when discipline feels heavy, when self-love is the last thing on your mind.

This book has a companion: The 100 Method Planner. It is the daily tool that brings everything in these pages to life. The book builds the belief. The planner delivers the practice. Together, they form a complete system for transformation. But each stands fully on its own. If you have the planner, use it. If not, the principles in this book are enough to begin.

One last thing before we start.

Whatever your goal is, your health, your creative work, your business, your relationships, your mind, this method was built for you. Not for a specific type of person or a specific kind of goal. For anyone who has something they want to build, change, or become. The only requirement is that you want it enough to show up for it.

One hundred days from now, you will be grateful you started today.

Let's begin.

BEFORE YOU BEGIN

How to set yourself up for 100 days of success

Before Part One begins, there is practical work to do. The ideas in this book matter. But ideas without preparation are just inspiration, and inspiration, as we have already established, is not enough. What follows is a brief but essential guide to setting yourself up before Day 1 arrives.

Do not skip this section. The decisions you make here will shape the quality of your entire 100 days.

How to Choose Your Goal

The most important decision of your 100 days is the one you make before they begin: choosing your goal. This decision deserves real thought, not hours of agonizing, but genuine reflection. The wrong goal will feel like a burden by Day 30. The right goal will feel like a calling, hard some days, but always worth returning to.

A strong 100-day goal has four qualities. First, it is specific. Not 'get healthier' but 'exercise for at least 45 minutes every day and eliminate processed sugar from my diet.' Not 'work on my business' but 'complete the first draft of my business plan and launch a simple website.' Specificity gives you something to act on, something to measure, and something to feel genuinely proud of when you achieve it.

Second, it is meaningful. The goal should connect to something you genuinely care about, not something you think you should want, not something that looks impressive to others, but something that, when you imagine achieving it, produces a real sense of excitement and purpose. If the goal doesn't move you, it won't carry you through the hard days. Choose something that matters.

Third, it is achievable within 100 days. This does not mean the goal should be small, it should be ambitious. But it should be realistic enough that 100 minutes of daily focused effort, consistently applied, can make meaningful progress. A goal so large that 10,000 minutes of effort would barely scratch the surface is not a 100-day goal. It is a multi-year goal that needs to be broken into 100-day chapters.

Fourth, it is singular. One goal. If you find yourself thinking 'I want to work on my health AND my business AND my creative project,' choose one. The others will be there in 100 days, and you will approach them with a proven system and a new sense of what you are capable of.

"The right goal doesn't just motivate you at the beginning. It calls you back on the hard days."

Setting Up Your Environment

Your environment is not neutral. It is either working with your 100-day commitment or against it. The way your physical space is arranged, the tools that are or aren't within reach, the people you spend time with, the apps on your phone, the schedule you keep, all of these things influence how easy or hard it is to show up for your 100 minutes every day.

Before Day 1, do a deliberate audit of your environment with a single question: does this make showing up easier or harder? Your workspace should be set up for your specific goal. If you are writing, your writing setup should be ready to go, laptop open, document open, notebook and pen within reach. If you are exercising, your workout clothes should be laid out the night before, your training space should be accessible, your equipment should be ready. Friction is the enemy of consistency. Reduce it wherever you can.

Your schedule is part of your environment. Before Day 1, decide exactly when your 100 minutes will happen. Morning is the most reliable window for most people, before the day's demands accumulate and before willpower depletes. But the best time is the one you will actually protect. Block it in your calendar. Treat it as an unmovable appointment. Let the people in your life know that this time is dedicated, so that the negotiation over whether it happens does not have to take place every single day.

Your digital environment matters too. If your 100 minutes will be spent in front of a screen, close every tab that is not directly related to your goal. Turn off notifications. Put your phone in another room if you can. The average person checks their phone 96 times a day, once every ten minutes. That rhythm is incompatible with the depth of focus your 100 minutes require. Protect the container.

The Night Before Day 1

The evening before your first day is more important than most people realize. It is the moment of final preparation, and it is also the moment when doubt tends to arrive most loudly.

Spend 20 minutes the night before Day 1 doing three things. Write your goal in full, not the abbreviated version, but the complete, specific statement of what you are committing to and why. Read it out loud. Hear yourself say it. This is not theater. It is the psychological act of making the commitment real.

Then set up your environment for the morning. Whatever needs to be in place for your first 100-minute session, put it there tonight. The less you have to decide in the morning, the better. Decision fatigue is real, and the fewer decisions your first session requires, the more likely you are to begin it with full energy and focus.

Finally, write a single sentence in your planner: what you intend to accomplish in your first 100 minutes. Not a detailed plan, just a clear intention. A direction. A starting point. Tomorrow, when you open the planner and see it, it will orient you immediately and eliminate the blank-page paralysis that can cost the first 20 minutes of a session.

You are ready. Day 1 begins tomorrow. Everything that follows, every chapter of this book, every principle it contains, is designed for the person you are about to become. Go to sleep knowing that.

A Note on Imperfection

Before the 100 days begin, make peace with this: they will not be perfect. There will be days that are harder than others. There will be sessions that feel unfocused, scattered, or inadequate. There will be moments when the goal feels too far away and the daily effort feels too small to matter.

These moments are not signs that something is wrong. They are the texture of a real journey. The 100 Method is not a promise of effortless progress. It is a structure for consistent effort, including the imperfect, uncomfortable, trying-anyway kind of effort that most people never get to experience because they stop before it becomes something.

The permission to be imperfect is not the permission to quit. It is the permission to continue. To show up on Day 37 with half the energy you had on Day 1 and do the 100 minutes anyway. To have a rough session on Day 58 and write an honest reflection about it in the planner instead of pretending it didn't happen. To be human, fallible, and fully committed, all at the same time.

That combination, human and committed, is what transformation is actually made of. Not perfection. Not unbroken streaks. Not flawless performance. Just the ongoing, imperfect, deeply courageous act of showing up.

Now, let's talk about why you're here in the first place. Part One begins on the next page.

01

THE CYCLE

Why we start strong and fade, and what that actually means about us

---

You have been here before.

The decision made. The energy high. The first few days, maybe even the first few weeks, filled with a sense of momentum that felt like it could carry you all the way to the finish line. And then, somewhere in the middle, something shifted. The fire dimmed. The routine that felt exciting started to feel like a burden. Life pushed in from the edges, and the goal, the goal you wanted so badly, quietly slipped to the back of the line.

If this sounds familiar, it is because it is almost universal. The starting-and-stopping cycle is not a sign of weakness, laziness, or lack of character. It is a predictable pattern, one that emerges when the way we approach goals does not account for how human beings actually work.

The Starting-Stopping Pattern

Most people begin a new goal with what feels like the most important ingredient: motivation. They are inspired, energized, and genuinely ready to make something happen. And for a while, that motivation carries them. The early days have a kind of electricity to them, everything feels possible, effort feels relatively easy, and progress, even when small, feels thrilling.

But motivation has a shelf life. It is designed to initiate, not to sustain. The neurological burst of excitement that comes with starting something new is real, dopamine rises in anticipation of reward, but it is not built to last indefinitely. As the novelty fades, as the effort required becomes clearer, as the gap between where you are and where you want to be becomes more apparent rather than less, motivation begins to recede.

This is not failure. This is biology.

The problem is that most people interpret the fading of motivation as a signal that something is wrong, with the goal, with themselves, with the timing. They conclude that if they were truly committed, if they really wanted it, the motivation would stay. And so when it goes, they go with it.

This is the cycle. And it repeats, not because people lack desire, but because they are relying on the wrong engine.

"Motivation is the spark. Discipline is the fuel. The 100 Method runs on fuel."

The Motivation Myth

We have been taught, implicitly and explicitly, that the key to achieving goals is finding the right motivation. Find your why. Connect to your purpose. Visualize the outcome. And while none of these things are wrong, clarity of purpose matters deeply, they are incomplete. They address the beginning of the journey but offer nothing for the middle.

The middle is where transformation actually happens. The middle is Days 30 through 70, when the novelty has worn off, when progress feels slow, when the initial excitement has settled into the quieter, less glamorous reality of daily effort. The middle is where most people stop. And it is precisely where The 100 Method is designed to hold you.

Here is what the research on behavior change consistently shows: motivation does not create consistency. Consistency creates motivation. When you show up repeatedly, even when you don't feel like it, even when progress is hard to see, even when the goal feels distant, something shifts. The action itself becomes easier. The identity of someone who shows up begins to form. And as that identity solidifies, motivation returns, not as a fragile emotional state, but as a stable orientation toward the goal.

You do not wait for motivation. You build it. Through action, through consistency, through the accumulated evidence of showing up when it counted.

What the Cycle Is Really Telling You

If you have been caught in the starting-and-stopping cycle, it is not telling you that you are incapable. It is telling you that you have been using the wrong approach. Specifically, it is telling you three things.

First, you have been relying on motivation to carry you past the point where motivation runs out. Second, you may have been pursuing too many goals at once, dividing your energy across so many fronts that none of them ever received enough attention to gain real momentum. Third, you may not have had a clear enough structure, a daily practice that removes the question of whether you will show up and replaces it with the simple habit of doing.

The 100 Method addresses all three. It gives you a structure built for the middle, for the hard days, the uninspired days, the days when you have to show up on discipline alone. It asks you to commit to one goal. And it gives you a daily practice so clear and so simple that the decision to show up is made once, at the beginning, and then simply executed every day after.

The cycle ends not when you find better motivation, but when you build a better system.

02

THE NOISE

Too many goals, too many plans, too little progress

We live in the age of too much.

Too much information. Too many frameworks. Too many productivity systems, morning routines, habit stacks, and optimization strategies. We consume content about becoming better at a rate that far outpaces our ability to actually implement any of it. And somewhere in all of that noise, the goal, the real one, the one that actually matters, gets buried.

The problem is not that people don't know what they want. Most people have a remarkably clear sense of the life they are trying to build. The problem is that they are trying to build all of it at once. And in doing so, they build none of it.

The Trap of Too Many Goals

Consider the average goal list. Health goals. Career goals. Relationship goals. Financial goals. Creative goals. Personal development goals. Each one legitimate. Each one genuinely desired. And collectively, an impossible ask.

Research on attention and cognitive load consistently shows that the human mind is not designed for parallel processing of complex goals. When we pursue multiple significant goals simultaneously, we do not give each one a proportional share of our attention. Instead, we give each one a fragmented, insufficient share, enough to feel like we are working on everything, not enough to make meaningful progress on anything.

The result is a particular kind of exhaustion. Not the satisfying exhaustion that comes from deep, focused work. But the draining fatigue of effort without progress. Of running hard and staying still. Of being busy in a way that never tips over into becoming.

This is the trap of too many goals. And it is not fixed by better time management or more efficient scheduling. It is fixed by radical focus.

The Power of One

One goal changes everything.

Not because one goal is more manageable, though it is. But because one goal, pursued with full commitment, has a compounding quality that multiple goals never achieve. Progress on a single goal accelerates. Clarity deepens. Identity shifts in a specific, powerful direction. And the confidence that grows from genuine progress on one thing becomes the fuel for the next goal after that.

Think of it this way. Sunlight spread across a field warms the ground. Sunlight focused through a lens ignites a fire. The energy is the same. The focus is different. And the results are incomparable.

The 100 Method asks you to be the lens. To take all of the energy, attention, and intention that you have been spreading across multiple goals and focus it, completely, unapologetically, on one. For 100 days. One hundred minutes a day.

This is not settling. It is strategy. It is the recognition that the fastest way to get everything you want is to pursue one thing at a time, with everything you have.

"You don't need more goals. You need more commitment to fewer of them."

Choosing Your One Goal

This is where many people hesitate. Choosing one goal feels like abandoning the others. Like admitting that some things don't matter. But that is not what it means.

Your other goals are not going anywhere. They will be there when your 100 days are done. And here is what you will find when you return to them: you will approach them differently. With more confidence. With a proven system. With the knowledge that you are someone who can commit to something and see it through.

Your one goal for the next 100 days should meet three criteria. It should be specific enough that you know, at the end of each day, whether you made progress or not. It should be meaningful enough that it is worth 100 minutes of your focused attention every single day. And it should be singular enough that 100 minutes a day is genuinely sufficient to move it forward.

Health. Creative work. Business. Mindset. Relationships. Any of these can be a 100-day goal. The method works because the framework is the constant, not the goal.

03

THE BROKEN PROMISE

What happens when we stop keeping our word to ourselves

Every time you set a goal and don't follow through, something happens that goes deeper than the missed goal itself.

You make a withdrawal from your self-trust account.

The goal itself may be forgotten within weeks. The resolution may fade from memory. But the quiet, often unconscious record of promises made and broken, that remains. It accumulates. And over time, it shapes the most important story you tell: the story of who you are and what you are capable of.

The Self-Trust Crisis

Self-trust is the foundation of every meaningful achievement. It is the internal belief that when you commit to something, you will follow through. That your word to yourself means something. That you are someone who can be counted on, by yourself.

When this trust is intact, goals feel achievable. Effort feels worthwhile. The gap between intention and action is small. But when self-trust has been eroded, by years of starting and stopping, of committing and retreating, of ambitious beginnings and quiet abandonments, that gap widens. Goals start to feel like wishful thinking. Commitment starts to feel like a setup for disappointment. And the protective mechanism that kicks in, the voice that says 'why bother, you'll just quit anyway' — is not laziness. It is self-preservation in the face of repeated disappointment.

This is the self-trust crisis. And it is more common than anyone likes to admit.

The Cost of Broken Promises

Consider what happens, neurologically and psychologically, each time we fail to keep a commitment to ourselves. The prefrontal cortex, responsible for planning, decision-making, and self-regulation, becomes slightly less confident in its own projections. Our predictions about our own behavior become less reliable. And reliability, the sense that we can be trusted to do what we say, is precisely what self-trust is built on.

The compounding effect works in reverse. Just as kept promises build trust, broken ones erode it. Not dramatically, not all at once, but incrementally, in the same quiet way that consistent action builds momentum, inconsistent action dissolves it.

The good news is this: the reverse is also true. Self-trust is not fixed. It is not a character trait you either have or don't. It is a skill, built through practice, through small kept commitments, through the accumulated experience of showing up when you said you would. And it can be rebuilt, one day at a time, over 100 days.

"The most important promise you will ever keep is the one you make to yourself."

Rebuilding the Account

This is what The 100 Method is, at its deepest level. Not just a system for achieving a goal, but a system for rebuilding the trust you have with yourself.

Every day that you complete your 100 minutes is a deposit. Not just toward the goal, but into the account of self-trust. Day by day, those deposits accumulate. By Day 25, you have 25 pieces of evidence that you keep your word. By Day 50, fifty. By Day 100, you have a hundred days of proof, proof that you are someone who commits and follows through. Proof that the story you've been telling yourself about your limitations was wrong.

That proof does not disappear when the 100 days end. It becomes part of who you are. It becomes the new baseline, the new definition of what you believe is possible for you. And it makes every subsequent goal easier, because you begin it already knowing, from direct experience, that you are someone who can do hard things.

This is why Day 100 is about so much more than the goal. The goal is the vehicle. The destination is a new relationship with yourself.

PART TWO

THE METHOD

---

100 minutes. 100 days. 1 goal. Here is why it works.

04

100 MINUTES

The science and psychology of deep, focused effort

One hundred minutes is not a random number.

It was chosen because it sits at a specific intersection, long enough to do meaningful work, short enough to be sustainable. Long enough to get past the warm-up phase of any task and into the deep, focused state where real progress happens. Short enough that it can fit into almost any schedule, any lifestyle, any life stage, if the commitment is real.

In a world that celebrates busyness, 100 minutes of intentional daily effort is a radical act. It is the rejection of scattered activity in favor of deliberate practice. It is the choice to go deep rather than wide, to do one thing well rather than many things adequately.

Why 100 Minutes Works

Research on human performance and focused work consistently points to a critical threshold. Below a certain duration of sustained attention, we never fully enter the state of deep engagement where genuine progress on complex goals becomes possible. We stay at the surface, responsive, reactive, busy, but not truly productive in the transformative sense.

One hundred minutes crosses that threshold. It is long enough to get past the initial resistance that accompanies any demanding task. Long enough to experience the shift, that moment, usually around 20 to 30 minutes in, when the mind settles, distraction fades, and genuine engagement begins. And long enough, once that engagement is established, for real work to happen.

At the same time, 100 minutes is short enough to be mentally sustainable day after day. It does not require the kind of heroic, all-day effort that most people cannot maintain without burning out. It asks for focused intensity for a defined period, after which the pressure releases. This balance, deep engagement within a manageable container, is what makes the daily 100-minute practice something you can sustain across 100 days rather than something that collapses after a week.

How to Structure Your 100 Minutes

There is no single right way to spend your 100 minutes, but there are structures that work better than others for most people.

The most common and effective approach is to break the 100 minutes into blocks. Four blocks of 25 minutes, with short breaks between each, mirrors the natural rhythm of human attention and allows the mind to sustain high-quality focus across the full duration. Two blocks of 50 minutes works well for tasks that require longer periods of sustained concentration, writing, deep analytical work, creative flow states. One unbroken 100-minute session suits those with strong focus discipline and tasks that build momentum over time.

The structure matters less than the consistency. What you are building is not just the skill of focusing for 100 minutes. You are building the daily habit of showing up for your goal with your full attention, for a defined and protected period of time. That habit, that daily practice of intentional engagement, is the engine of the method.

"100 minutes a day is not a lot of time. But compounded over 100 days, it is everything."

Making Your 100 Minutes Sacred

The most important decision you will make about your 100 minutes is not how to structure them, but how to protect them.

In a life full of competing demands, notifications, obligations, and the endless noise of modern existence, 100 minutes of focused time does not happen by accident. It happens by decision, and then by defense of that decision, every single day.

This means choosing a time that works consistently. For most people, the morning is most reliable, before the day's demands accumulate and willpower is freshest. But the best time is the one that you will actually protect. Evening works if that is genuinely when you are most able to focus. Midday works if your schedule allows. The time is less important than the consistency.

It also means reducing friction. Set up your environment so that your 100 minutes are easy to begin. Put your tools in place the night before. Close the browser tabs. Silence the phone. Tell the people around you what this time is for. The less decision-making required at the start of your 100 minutes, the easier it will be to show up for them day after day.

And it means treating the 100 minutes like the non-negotiable appointment that it is. Not something that happens if everything else cooperates. Not something that gets pushed when life gets busy. The one thing that happens, regardless of what else the day brings.

THE 100 TAKEAWAY

100 minutes a day is not a lot of time. But compounded over 100 days, it is everything.

05

100 DAYS

Why 100 days is the perfect length of a transformation

Thirty days is not enough.

A 30-day challenge can build a habit. It can create momentum. It can prove something to yourself in a limited, provisional way. But it rarely goes deep enough to change who you are. The transformation that 30 days produces is real, but it is fragile, easily undone by a return to old patterns, old environments, old ways of thinking about yourself.

A full year is too long. Not because the transformation isn't worth a year, often it is. But because a year lacks urgency. When the finish line is 365 days away, the cost of a missed day feels negligible. The pressure that drives consistent effort diffuses across too large a span of time, and the motivation to show up on any given day weakens accordingly.

One hundred days is the answer. It is long enough to produce genuine, durable change. Long enough to move through multiple phases of transformation, the excitement of beginning, the grind of the middle, the breakthrough of sustained effort, and the identity shift that comes from seeing it through. And short enough that every day matters. Short enough that the finish line is always visible.

The Four Phases of 100 Days

Every 100-day journey moves through four distinct phases. Understanding them in advance does not make them easier, exactly, but it makes them navigable. It means that when you hit the grind of the middle, you know it is coming, you know it is temporary, and you know what lies on the other side.

Days 1 through 25 are the Ignition Phase. Everything is new. The commitment is fresh, the energy is high, and the daily practice has not yet had time to feel routine. Progress is visible and motivating. Showing up feels relatively easy, because novelty is doing some of the work for you. The goal in this phase is to establish the habit, to make the 100 minutes a fixed, non-negotiable part of your day before the novelty fades.

Days 26 through 50 are the Grind. The novelty is gone. The habit may or may not be solidly established. Progress is slower, harder to see, and less immediately rewarding. This is the phase where most people quit, not because the goal has become unachievable, but because the gap between effort and visible reward feels too wide. This is the phase The 100 Method was built for. The structure holds you when feeling won't.

Days 51 through 75 mark the Shift. Something changes in this phase, often subtly at first, then more noticeably. The daily practice starts to feel like part of who you are rather than something you are doing. Progress becomes more visible, sometimes dramatically so. A sense of momentum returns, but it is different from the early momentum, steadier, more grounded, built on weeks of sustained effort rather than the electricity of a new beginning.

Days 76 through 100 are the Identity phase. You are no longer becoming someone who pursues this goal. You are that person. The daily 100 minutes is not something you have to remember to do. It is what you do. And the finish line — Day 100 — is not an ending. It is a confirmation. Evidence, carved out across 100 days of real life, of who you have become.

"You don't need a lifetime to change. You need 100 days of decision."

What to Do When It Gets Hard

It will get hard. Usually around Days 30 to 50. The initial excitement has faded, the daily practice may feel more like obligation than opportunity, and the voice of doubt, which was quiet at the beginning, starts to get louder.

This is the moment the method proves its worth. Because the answer, when it gets hard, is the same as it has always been: show up. Do the 100 minutes. Not perfectly. Not with full energy or optimal focus. Just show up and do the work, because the day you are most tempted to quit is often the day before something shifts.

The 100-day framework helps here in a specific way. When you are on Day 38 and you don't want to continue, the finish line — Day 100 — is close enough to be real. You can count the days that remain. And the days you have already completed are evidence — 37 days of proof that you can do this. The math works in your favor. You have already done the hard part of beginning. You already have momentum. The effort required to continue is less than the effort already spent.

Count what you have built, not just what remains.

You don't need a lifetime to change. You need 100 days of decision.

06

1 GOAL

The transformative power of choosing one thing and meaning it

---

The most countercultural thing this book asks of you is also the most powerful.

One goal.

In a world that constantly pushes you toward more, more goals, more optimization, more productivity, more ambition across more dimensions of life simultaneously, choosing one goal feels almost transgressive. Like you are settling. Like you are leaving something on the table.

You are not settling. You are focusing. And there is a world of difference between the two.

Why One Goal Is Not Settling

Settling implies giving up on something you wanted. Focusing implies directing your full energy toward something you want completely. These are opposite orientations, and the results they produce are incomparable.

When you choose one goal for your 100 days, you are not saying that your other goals don't matter. You are saying that this goal matters enough to receive your full attention. And full attention, genuine, sustained, daily attention, is what produces the kind of progress that compounds into transformation.

Consider what 100 minutes a day, for 100 days, totals. That is 10,000 minutes. Almost 167 hours of focused, intentional effort on a single goal. Applied consistently, that volume of deliberate practice does not just move the needle, it changes the game. It takes someone from beginner to competent. From competent to capable. From capable to someone who has genuinely developed a skill, built a body of work, transformed a habit, or shifted the trajectory of their health, career, or creative life.

That is what one goal, pursued with full commitment, produces. And it is only possible when the attention is not divided.

The Identity Question

There is a deeper reason to choose one goal, and it has nothing to do with efficiency.

The goal you choose for your 100 days is not just a target. It is a statement about who you are becoming. When you commit to a health goal, you are not just trying to lose weight or build strength. You are becoming someone for whom physical wellbeing is a priority, someone who treats their body as an investment rather than an afterthought. When you commit to a creative goal, you are not just trying to finish a project. You are becoming someone who creates, who shows up for their craft with discipline and devotion.

This identity shift is one of the most powerful and lasting effects of The 100 Method. The goal may be achieved or not fully achieved by Day 100. But the identity, the lived experience of being someone who shows up, who commits, who follows through, that is durable. That persists. And it becomes the foundation for every goal that follows.

"One goal, fully pursued, will do more for your life than ten goals half-heartedly chased."

Committing Without Reservation

Once you have chosen your goal, commit to it without reservation. Not provisionally. Not with a mental escape clause that says you can quit if it gets too hard. Fully. Completely. With the understanding that for the next 100 days, this goal is the priority.

The contract in The 100 Method Planner is not a formality. It is a psychological anchor. Research on commitment and follow-through consistently shows that written, stated, and formally made commitments produce higher rates of follow-through than mental intentions. The act of writing your goal, stating your commitment, and signing your name is not symbolic. It is structural. It creates a reference point, a moment you can return to when doubt arises and remind yourself: I decided this. I chose this. I am doing this.

Doubt will arrive. It always does. The commitment is not a guarantee that doubt won't come. It is a structure that makes it easier to continue despite the doubt, because you have already made the decision, and the decision stands.

THE 100 TAKEAWAY

One goal, fully pursued, will do more for your life than ten goals half-heartedly chased.

PART THREE

THE FOUR PILLARS

The foundation that holds everything up

07

ACCOUNTABILITY

The honest relationship you build with yourself

Accountability has a reputation problem.

For most people, the word conjures something punitive, a system of surveillance, judgment, and consequences for falling short. An external force that watches what you do and holds you responsible when you fail. This version of accountability is fear-based, and it tends to produce one of two results: either rigid compliance that collapses the moment the external pressure is removed, or avoidance, the quiet decision to simply not commit to anything that could be judged.

The 100 Method is built on a different understanding of accountability entirely.

Accountability as Truth-Telling

Real accountability is not surveillance. It is honesty. It is the practice of seeing yourself clearly, your actions, your patterns, your choices, without flinching, and without the elaborate stories we tell ourselves to explain why we aren't doing the things we said we would do.

This kind of accountability is not about punishment. It is about information. Did you show up today or didn't you? Not why you didn't show up, not the extenuating circumstances, not the complicated justification, just the simple, factual answer. Yes or no. This honesty, practiced daily, becomes one of the most powerful tools for change available to you.

Because what you can see clearly, you can change. And what you hide, from others or from yourself, you cannot.

Internal vs. External Accountability

External accountability, checking in with a partner, reporting to a group, paying a coach, can be helpful, especially in the early days of a new commitment. The knowledge that someone else knows what you said you would do adds a layer of social motivation that can carry you through moments when internal motivation flags.

But external accountability has a ceiling. It works while the external pressure is present and stops working when it is removed. The goal of The 100 Method is not to create dependence on external accountability, but to build internal accountability, the kind that persists even when no one is watching. The kind that holds you to your commitment because you hold yourself to your commitment.

This is harder to build, but infinitely more durable. And it is built the same way everything else in this method is built, through daily practice. Each time you honestly assess your day in your planner, each time you mark whether you showed up or not without softening the truth, you are developing the muscle of internal accountability. Slowly, then powerfully, it becomes a natural way of relating to yourself.

"You cannot grow beyond what you are willing to honestly see."

Accountability on the Hard Days

The real test of accountability is not on the good days, when everything goes according to plan and the 100 minutes happen easily and the reflection at the end of the day is satisfying. The test is on the hard days. The days when you didn't show up, or showed up halfway, or showed up with your body while your mind was elsewhere.

On those days, the temptation is to soften the record. To write a justification instead of an honest assessment. To check the box anyway because technically you did something. Resist this. The integrity of the practice depends on the integrity of the record.

What you do with a hard day matters enormously. Not punishing yourself, that is not accountability, that is self-sabotage. But acknowledging it honestly, understanding what happened without hiding behind excuses, and making a clear commitment to what tomorrow looks like. That is accountability. And practiced consistently, it is one of the most profound forces for growth available to any human being.

08

CONSISTENCY

Showing up when the feeling is gone

Consistency is the least glamorous of the four pillars. It does not announce itself. It does not produce dramatic moments of inspiration or sudden, visible transformation. It works quietly, incrementally, in the background, showing up in the small gap between who you were yesterday and who you are today.

And yet it is the pillar that everything else rests on.

Without consistency, accountability becomes a one-time event rather than a practice. Discipline becomes a burst of effort rather than a way of being. Self-love becomes a nice idea rather than a lived commitment. Consistency is what converts intention into identity, what takes the goal from something you want and makes it something you are building, day after relentless day.

What Consistency Actually Is

Consistency is not perfection. This distinction is critical, and it is one that trips up an enormous number of people.

Perfectionism says: if I cannot do this perfectly, I should not do it at all. If I miss a day, the streak is broken and the whole effort is compromised. If my 100 minutes were distracted and unfocused, they don't count. This is the mindset that turns one missed day into two, and two into a week, and a week into a quiet abandonment of the goal.

Consistency says something different. It says: I show up. Not perfectly, not always at my best, not always with the energy or focus I would like. But I show up. Because the pattern of showing up, the identity of someone who keeps coming back, is more valuable than any single session, no matter how good.

The research on habit formation is clear on this point. Missing one day has no measurable impact on the formation of a habit. What matters is the overall pattern, the consistent return after every absence, however brief. The practice is not destroyed by a missed day. It is only destroyed by the decision that a missed day means it is over.

Building the Pattern

Consistency is easier to maintain when it is embedded in structure. The decision of whether to show up should ideally be made once, at the beginning of the 100 days, rather than re-made every single morning. When showing up becomes a non-negotiable, the daily question shifts from 'will I do this?' to 'how will I do this today?'

Environment plays a significant role in this. Your surroundings are either working with your consistency or against it. A workspace that is set up for your 100-minute practice invites you in. A schedule that has a designated time for your daily work removes the question of when. Habits that anchor your practice, a cup of coffee before you begin, a specific playlist, a simple ritual that signals to your mind that it is time, reduce the friction between the intention to show up and the act of showing up.

None of this makes consistency automatic. But it makes it easier. And easier, compounded across 100 days, makes all the difference.

"You don't rise to the level of your goals. You fall to the level of your consistency."

Consistency as Self-Respect

There is a dimension to consistency that goes beyond strategy and habit architecture, and it is this: every time you show up for your 100 minutes, you are casting a vote. Not just for the goal, but for yourself. You are saying, through action rather than words, that

you are worth showing up for. That your goal is worth the effort.
That the person you are becoming is worth the investment of
today's time and energy.

Repeated enough times, those votes accumulate into a new self-
image. Not the self-image of someone who tries and quits, who
starts and stops, who wants things but doesn't follow through.
The self-image of someone who shows up. Someone who, when
they say they are going to do something, does it. Someone who
has proven, across 100 days of real life, that they can be counted
on by the most important person in their world: themselves.

That self-image is the most valuable thing The 100 Method
produces. The goal is the vehicle. The self-image is the
destination.

09

DISCIPLINE

Freedom in disguise

Discipline has been misunderstood.

It has been positioned as the opposite of freedom, a cage of obligations and restrictions, a life of doing what you should rather than what you want. People resist discipline not because they are lazy, but because they have been taught to associate it with deprivation, with rigidity, with the joyless suppression of everything spontaneous and human.

This is wrong. Profoundly, consequentially wrong.

Discipline, practiced correctly, is the most direct path to freedom available to any person. Not freedom from effort, but freedom from the weight of unfinished business, unkept promises, and the nagging awareness of what you could be building but aren't. The discipline of daily focused work is what creates the conditions for everything else, the confidence, the progress, the identity, the life, that you actually want.

Redefining Discipline

Think about the moments in your life when you have felt most free. Not the moments of passive consumption or idle escape, though those have their place, but the moments of genuine aliveness. When you created something. When you achieved something difficult. When you pushed past what you thought you were capable of and found something unexpected on the other side.

Those moments are almost always the product of discipline. Of the repeated choice to do the work, to show up, to continue past the point where comfort was available. The discipline was the price. The freedom, the expanded sense of what is possible, the deep satisfaction of genuine achievement, was the return.

Discipline is not the opposite of freedom. It is the gateway to it.

Discipline in Practice

The practical reality of discipline in the context of The 100 Method is this: there will be days when you do not want to do your 100 minutes. When you are tired, uninspired, distracted, or simply resistant in a way that has no clear cause. These days are not exceptions. They are the rule. They are the days that the practice was built for.

On those days, discipline is the bridge between intention and action. It does not require that you feel like working. It does not require that the conditions be perfect or that the energy be high. It requires only that you begin. Because the beginning is where discipline does its most important work.

Research on motivation and action consistently shows that the relationship between feeling and doing is far more bidirectional than we typically assume. We tend to think that motivation leads to action, that we need to feel ready before we begin. But the evidence shows that action leads to motivation just as reliably. Begin the work, and the engagement follows. Open the notebook, start the session, make the first move, and the resistance that felt insurmountable from the outside frequently dissolves once you are actually in it.

Discipline is the commitment to begin, regardless of how beginning feels.

"Every act of discipline is a vote for the person you are in the process of becoming."

The Long Game

The deepest benefit of discipline is not what it produces in a single session or even across a single 100-day journey. It is what it produces over a lifetime of application.

Every time you choose the work over the excuse, you are doing two things simultaneously. You are making progress on the goal in front of you. And you are becoming someone for whom that choice is more natural, someone for whom the gap between intention and action is a little smaller, the resistance a little lighter, the default a little more reliably toward doing rather than avoiding.

This is the compounding return on discipline. Not just the goal achieved, but the person shaped by the pursuit of it. The 100 days will end. The discipline you build in them, the practice, the identity, the deeply ingrained habit of choosing effort over ease, will remain. And it will make everything that comes after easier, because you will approach it as someone who already knows how to do hard things.

THE 100 TAKEAWAY

Every act of discipline is a vote for the person you are in the process of becoming.

10

SELF-LOVE

The foundation that makes everything else possible

Self-love is the pillar most likely to be misunderstood, undervalued, or quietly dismissed by people who consider themselves serious about achievement.

It sounds soft. Optional. Like something you address after the goal is achieved, as a reward for the hard work. But this gets it exactly backwards.

Self-love is not the reward at the end of the journey. It is the fuel for the journey itself. Without it, accountability becomes self-punishment. Consistency becomes compulsion. Discipline becomes deprivation. The entire framework collapses into something joyless and unsustainable, not transformation, but a grind that produces exhaustion rather than growth.

What Self-Love Actually Is

Self-love is not self-indulgence. It is not the permission to skip your 100 minutes because you are tired, or to lower your standards because the goal is hard. It is not the soft voice that says 'it's okay, you don't have to' every time the work gets uncomfortable.

Self-love is the deep, foundational belief that you are worth investing in. That your goals matter. That the person you are becoming is worth the effort of today. That you deserve the life you are working toward, not as a distant reward for perfect performance, but as an expression of what you already know yourself to be: someone worthy of growth, of achievement, of the best of what life can offer.

From that foundation, everything else becomes possible. Accountability is not punitive, it is caring. Consistency is not rigid, it is an expression of how much you value your own development. Discipline is not deprivation, it is the deepest act of self-respect available to you.

Self-Love on the Hard Days

The 100 days will contain hard days. Days when nothing goes according to plan. Days when the 100 minutes are a struggle from beginning to end. Days when you look at your planner and feel something closer to shame than pride.

On those days, self-love is not the voice that lets you off the hook. It is the voice that holds you with both firmness and gentleness simultaneously. It says: you struggled today, and that is real. And tomorrow you will show up again. Not because you have to. Because you are worth showing up for.

This is the practice of self-love in the context of transformation: the ability to acknowledge difficulty without making it mean something terrible about you. The ability to have a hard day without having a hard identity. The ability to be human, imperfect, inconsistent, sometimes struggling, without withdrawing the basic respect and care you owe yourself.

"You are worth every minute of this. Don't let anyone, including yourself, convince you otherwise."

Why Self-Love Is the Foundation

Consider what happens to accountability, consistency, and discipline when self-love is absent.

Accountability becomes self-criticism, a harsh, punitive audit of everything that fell short, rather than an honest assessment that leads to growth. Consistency becomes pressure, a relentless demand for perfect performance that makes any deviation feel like catastrophic failure. Discipline becomes self-punishment, a way of forcing yourself to do things rather than choosing them from a place of genuine commitment to your own wellbeing.

None of that is sustainable. And none of it is what The 100 Method asks of you.

What it asks is harder and simpler than perfection. It asks you to care about yourself enough to show up. To believe that your goal is worth pursuing because you are worth pursuing. To bring the same warmth and commitment to your own development that you would bring to someone you love deeply.

You are doing this because you matter. That is the whole foundation. Everything else is built on it.

You are worth every minute of this. Don't let anyone, including yourself, convince you otherwise.

PART FOUR

THE METHOD IN ACTION

What 100 days looks like across every kind of goal

THE METHOD IN ACTION

The 100 Method is universal. It does not belong to any single goal type, any particular demographic, or any specific vision of what a transformed life looks like. It belongs to anyone with a goal worth pursuing and the willingness to pursue it with full commitment for 100 days.

The next four chapters bring the method to life across different goal categories, health, creative work, business, and mindset. Each chapter follows the arc of a real 100-day journey: what it looks like at the beginning, what happens in the middle when it gets hard, and what becomes possible by the end.

You will find yourself in at least one of these chapters. And what you will find there is not a guarantee, transformation is never a guarantee, but a map. A picture of what is possible when you bring 100 minutes, 100 days, and one goal into full alignment with the life you are trying to build.

11

HEALTH & BODY

What 100 days of intentional physical effort creates

The health goal is perhaps the most common 100-day commitment, and the one with the highest early dropout rate. Not because people don't want to improve their health, but because they approach it in a way that is almost guaranteed to fail: all-or-nothing intensity followed by inevitable burnout.

The 100 Method offers a different architecture entirely.

What a Health-Focused 100 Days Looks Like

Your health goal for the next 100 days might be building a consistent exercise practice. It might be transforming your nutrition, improving your sleep, building strength, increasing your energy, or simply developing a daily relationship with your body that is caring rather than adversarial. Whatever the specific goal, the framework is the same: 100 minutes of intentional, daily focus.

In the early days, this might mean a 45-minute workout followed by 30 minutes of meal planning and 25 minutes of learning, reading about nutrition, researching approaches, understanding your body better. Or it might be a full 100 minutes of movement, broken into two sessions. The specific structure matters less than the consistency of the practice and the quality of the attention.

The first 25 days are about building the habit. Your body is adapting, your schedule is adjusting, and the novelty of the new routine is carrying more of the load than it will later. This is the time to establish the daily practice so firmly that it becomes automatic, so that the question is never whether you will do it, but simply what it will look like today.

The Middle — Where Health Goals Usually Die

Days 26 through 50 are the most vulnerable phase of a health-focused 100 days. The initial results, the energy boost, the early physical changes, the excitement of a new routine, have settled into a baseline. Progress is still happening, but it is slower and less dramatic than the beginning. The body is adapting in ways that are real but not always visible.

This is where most people quit. Not because the approach isn't working, but because it doesn't look like it's working from the outside. The scale might be plateauing. The strength gains might be slowing. The discipline required to keep showing up feels disproportionate to the results you can see.

The 100 Method holds you through this phase with structure. You show up for your 100 minutes not because you can see the results today, but because you made a commitment and the commitment stands. And what the science of physiological adaptation tells us is that the changes happening in the middle, often invisible on the outside, are some of the most fundamental. Cardiovascular efficiency improving. Muscle fiber developing. Metabolic processes shifting. The body recomposing itself, quietly, while you show up every day and do the work.

The Shift — What Day 100 Produces

By Day 75, something has changed. Not just in the body, though the physical changes by this point are often significant, but in the identity. You are no longer someone who is trying to get healthy. You are someone who takes care of their body. Every day. Without significant deliberation.

The health habit, at this stage, has crossed a threshold. It is no longer effortful in the way it was at the beginning. It is simply part of who you are and what you do. The 100 minutes of daily focus has become a practice, one that continues past Day 100 not because you are forcing it, but because it is now genuinely part of your life.

By Day 100, the physical results are real and measurable. But the more lasting gift is the identity. You are someone who shows up for their health, every day, regardless of how they feel. That identity, that self-image, persists long after the 100 days are over and becomes the foundation for every subsequent health goal.

"Your body keeps score. And so does your confidence."

THE 100 TAKEAWAY

The body transforms from the outside in. The identity transforms from the inside out. Both are happening in your 100 days.

12

CREATIVE WORK

What 100 days of showing up for your craft unlocks

Creative work has a particular relationship with resistance.

No other category of human endeavor is quite so skilled at generating reasons not to begin. The conditions aren't right. The idea isn't fully formed. The inspiration hasn't arrived. The project is too ambitious, or not ambitious enough, or it's too early, or it's too late. Creative resistance is sophisticated and relentless, and it has claimed more potential work than any external obstacle ever could.

The 100 Method dismantles creative resistance by removing the most dangerous variable: choice. When you have committed to 100 minutes of creative work every day for 100 days, the question of whether to create is no longer on the table. The question is only what to create today, and then you begin.

The First 25 Days of Creative Work

The early days of a creative 100-day commitment are often characterized by imperfection. What comes out in the first few weeks may not be your best work. It may feel rough, tentative, or far from the vision in your head. This is not only normal, it is necessary.

Creative capacity, like physical capacity, builds through use. The daily practice of showing up and creating, regardless of the quality of what emerges, develops creative fluency. It trains the mind to generate ideas more readily, to move from blank page to engaged work more quickly, to access the creative state with less of the friction that characterized the early sessions.

By Day 25, something usually shifts. The warm-up period of each session shortens. The quality of the work begins to climb. And more importantly, the identity of someone who creates daily, someone for whom creative work is not a special occasion but a daily practice, begins to solidify.

The Body of Work

One of the most tangible and often surprising outcomes of a creative 100-day commitment is the sheer volume of work produced. When you write 100 minutes every day for 100 days, you write. When you paint 100 minutes every day for 100 days, you paint. When you compose, design, build, or develop, you produce a body of work that is substantial, varied, and often far more significant than anything produced in the scattered, inspiration-dependent creative sessions that precede the commitment.

This body of work is its own kind of proof. It is the material evidence that you create, not when you feel like it, not when the conditions are perfect, not when inspiration strikes, but every single day, because you are someone who creates. The identity precedes the feeling. The practice precedes the inspiration. And the body of work that emerges is the record of a creative life actually lived, rather than endlessly imagined.

> *"The muse rewards the consistent, not the inspired."*

Show up for your creative work every day, and the creative work will show up for you.

13

BUSINESS & CAREER

What 100 focused days can do for your professional life

The professional world rewards focus. It always has.

Not the appearance of busyness, which is everywhere and produces less than people imagine. But genuine, sustained, strategic focus on the thing that matters most. The kind of focus that builds skills, produces results, and creates the compounding advantages that separate people who move forward from people who stay still.

One hundred minutes a day of focused professional effort, applied to a single goal for 100 days, is enough to launch something significant. Not everything, but something real, something measurable, something that would not have existed without the commitment.

Choosing Your Professional Goal

A business or career goal for a 100-day commitment might be launching a product or service. Building a professional skill. Growing an audience or client base. Writing the business plan that has been sitting in your head for years. Making the career transition you have been postponing. Developing the expertise that would make you genuinely competitive in your field.

Whatever it is, the criterion is the same as for any 100-day goal: it should be specific enough to make daily progress measurable, meaningful enough to be worth 100 minutes of daily focused attention, and singular enough that 100 minutes is sufficient to move it forward in a meaningful way.

One hundred minutes a day of focused business effort is, in many respects, more productive than a full day of unfocused work. Research on cognitive performance and decision quality consistently shows that mental resources deplete across the course of a day. The focused professional who protects 100 minutes of high-quality attention for their most important work early in the day will typically outproduce the person who spends eight hours in a reactive, distracted state.

What 100 Days Builds Professionally

The professional results of a 100-day commitment vary by goal, but the pattern is consistent. What begins as daily incremental progress accumulates into something substantial. The skill that seemed distant at Day 1 is genuinely developing by Day 50. The project that seemed overwhelming at the beginning is complete, or nearly so, by Day 100. The professional identity, the sense of being someone who is actively building something, growing something, becoming something in their career, has shifted in ways that are both internally experienced and externally visible.

There is also a confidence effect that is specific to professional 100-day commitments. When you spend 100 days showing up for your professional development, your relationship to your own capabilities changes. You have evidence, not just belief or hope, but actual evidence, produced through daily effort, of what you can learn, build, and achieve. That evidence changes how you show up in professional contexts. In meetings, in negotiations, in conversations about what you are capable of. You are no longer someone hoping to grow professionally. You are someone who knows, from direct experience, that they can.

"Clarity of focus is your greatest competitive advantage."

14

MINDSET & PERSONAL GROWTH

What 100 days of inner work produces

The most invisible transformation is often the most profound.

When your 100-day goal is internal, shifting a mindset, developing a daily reflective practice, working through patterns that have held you back, building emotional resilience, cultivating a relationship with yourself that is more honest and more compassionate than the one that came before, the results don't show up in before-and-after photos or measurable performance metrics. They show up in the quality of your thinking, the tone of your internal dialogue, the speed at which you recover from setbacks, and the growing sense that you are no longer at the mercy of your own mind.

These are some of the most valuable changes a human being can make. And they are among the hardest to sustain without a daily structure like the one The 100 Method provides.

Inner Work as a 100-Day Goal

A mindset or personal growth goal might look like a daily journaling practice. It might be meditation, therapy, reading and reflection, working through a specific pattern of thought or behavior that has been limiting you. It might be developing emotional intelligence, building resilience, or cultivating the kind of stillness and self-awareness that allows you to respond to life rather than react to it.

The 100 minutes for this kind of goal might be structured differently than for a physical or professional goal. Forty minutes of reading or learning, 30 minutes of journaling or reflection, 30 minutes of meditation or intentional practice. Or some variation that fits the specific nature of the inner work being done. The structure is less prescribed here, because inner work is more personal than any other category, but the commitment is the same: 100 minutes, every day, devoted to your inner life.

The Invisible Transformation

By Day 50 of a mindset-focused 100-day commitment, something has shifted, not in the external circumstances of your life, but in your relationship to those circumstances. The reactive patterns that used to pull you into conflict, anxiety, or self-doubt are still there, patterns don't disappear in 50 days, but your relationship to them has changed. You see them more clearly. You have a practice for working with them. You are no longer entirely at their mercy.

By Day 100, the inner landscape has genuinely changed. The change may be subtle from the outside, but from the inside it is unmistakable. You think differently. You talk to yourself differently. The stories you tell about who you are and what is possible for you have shifted, quietly, incrementally, and then all at once, in the direction of something more true, more generous, and more expansive than what came before.

This is the specific gift of mindset work: it changes the filter through which you see everything else. A transformed mindset does not just improve the goal you were pursuing, it transforms your approach to every goal, every challenge, every relationship, every opportunity that follows. It is the investment with the widest return.

"The outer life is always a reflection of the inner work."

PART FIVE

YOUR 100 BEGINS

From reader to doer, the final step

15

THE DECISION

The only thing standing between you and Day 1

You have read the book. You understand the method. You know why 100 minutes works, why 100 days is the right container, why one goal is the right approach. You know the four pillars. You have seen the method in action across different kinds of goals.

And somewhere in the back of your mind, the voice is already present. The one that has been there every other time you have stood at this particular threshold.

Maybe after the weekend. Maybe when things settle down at work. Maybe when I have a clearer sense of which goal to choose. Maybe when I feel more ready.

Let's talk about that voice.

The Last Barrier

The voice is not your enemy. It is your fear, and fear, in this context, is often a sign that you are about to do something that matters. The things we approach without any resistance are rarely the things that change us. The things that change us are almost always accompanied by some version of that voice.

But the voice lies about one specific thing, and it is the lie that costs people the most. It says that readiness is a precondition for beginning. That you need to feel ready before you start. That there is a better moment, a clearer sense of purpose, a more optimal set of conditions waiting just around the corner.

There is not. The perfect moment is a myth maintained by the part of you that is afraid of what happens if you try and fall short.

The conditions will never be ideal. Life will always have competing demands, legitimate complications, and genuine reasons to postpone. And if you wait for the moment when all of those things resolve themselves, you will wait forever.

The decision to begin does not require readiness. It requires only willingness. The willingness to start before you feel ready, to commit before you feel certain, to take the first step before you can see the whole staircase.

What the Decision Actually Is

The decision to begin your 100 days is not primarily a decision about the goal. It is a decision about yourself.

It is the decision that you are worth showing up for. That your goal is worth 100 minutes of your daily attention. That the person you are becoming, the more capable, more confident, more self-trusting version of you that exists on the other side of 100 days, is worth the effort of today.

Every person who has ever transformed their life in a meaningful way made this decision. Not always dramatically. Not always with perfect clarity or full confidence. But they made it. They chose to begin. And the beginning, which felt uncertain and imperfect and not quite right, turned out to be exactly right. Because every beginning is imperfect. That is not a problem with the beginning. That is what beginnings are.

"The decision to begin is already an act of transformation. Make it."

Your Companion for the Journey

The 100 Method Planner is designed to be with you for every day of the next 100. It is where your commitment lives, signed and dated, in your own handwriting, as a record of the decision you are making today. It is where your daily intentions are set, your 100 minutes are tracked, your wins are recorded, and your reflections are captured. It is the daily structure that holds the method in place when motivation is inconsistent, when discipline is hard, when the middle of the journey feels longer than you expected.

If you do not yet have the planner, you can find it at thehundredmethod.com. If you have it in your hands right now, turn to the first page. Find the line that says 'This planner belongs to.' Write your name.

That is Day 1.

A Final Word

One hundred days from now, you will look back at this moment, the moment you decided, with a specific kind of gratitude. Not the gratitude of someone who found it easy, who never struggled, who moved through the 100 days without doubt or difficulty. But the gratitude of someone who chose to begin anyway. Who showed up even when it was hard. Who kept their word to themselves across 100 days of real life, with all of its complexity and resistance and ordinary difficulty.

That gratitude is waiting for you on the other side of this decision.

You have been ready for longer than you know.

Your 100 days start now.

THE 100 TAKEAWAY

The decision to begin is already an act of transformation. Make it.

FREQUENTLY ASKED QUESTIONS

Honest answers to the questions people actually ask

These are the questions that come up most often, before people begin their 100 days, in the middle when things get complicated, and at the end when they are thinking about what comes next. The answers are honest. Some of them may not be what you were hoping to hear.

What if I miss a day?

Missing a day does not end your 100-day commitment. It does not reset your count. It does not mean you have failed. It means you missed a day, and tomorrow, you show up again. The only thing that ends your 100 days is the decision to stop. One missed day is human. A pattern of missed days is a signal to look honestly at whether something needs to change in your approach, your schedule, or your commitment. But a single missed day? Show up tomorrow. Continue the count.

Can I change my goal midway through?

In most cases, no, and the reason matters. The impulse to change goals in the middle of a 100-day commitment is almost always the voice of resistance, not the voice of wisdom. The goal gets hard, the novelty has faded, and the mind begins looking for an exit that feels legitimate. Changing the goal is that exit dressed up as a reasonable decision. Stay with your original goal unless something genuinely fundamental has changed, a life circumstance that makes the goal truly no longer relevant or possible. If you are changing your goal because it got hard, stay with it. Hard is the point.

What counts as 100 minutes?

One hundred minutes of focused, intentional effort directly related to your goal. This means work, not thinking about work, not planning to work, not researching tangentially related topics. The 100 minutes should be active, engaged, and directed. If you are writing, you are writing. If you are exercising, you are exercising. If you are building your business, you are building. Preparation time, warm-up, and transition time do not count toward the 100 minutes. The measure is focused effort, and you know the difference between that and everything else.

What if 100 minutes is too much on some days?

Some days, life makes 100 minutes genuinely impossible. A family emergency. Illness. A day that simply falls apart in ways beyond your control. On those days, show up for whatever you can — 30 minutes, 50 minutes, even 20. Something is always better than nothing, and the act of showing up at all, even partially, maintains the identity of someone who shows up. Mark the day honestly in your planner. Note what happened and what you managed. Then make Day 100 minutes tomorrow non-negotiable.

Do I need the planner to do The 100 Method?

No. The method in this book is complete on its own. You can track your 100 minutes and your daily reflections in any notebook, any journal, any system that works for you. The planner is designed to make the practice as frictionless and structured as possible, with daily pages that guide you through intention-setting, focus tracking, reflection, and milestone check-ins. But the method is the method, regardless of what you use to record it.

What if my goal isn't achieved by Day 100?

This happens, and it does not mean the 100 days failed. Some goals are not fully achievable in 100 days, they require multiple 100-day commitments, each building on the last. What matters is that you made genuine progress, that you showed up consistently, and that you have 100 days of evidence that you are someone who pursues their goals with real commitment. That evidence is valuable regardless of where the goal stands on Day 100. Assess what was achieved, what was learned, and what the next 100 days need to look like. Then decide whether to continue with the same goal or move to the next one.

How do I stay motivated in the middle?

You don't, not in the traditional sense. Motivation in the middle of a 100-day commitment is unreliable at best and absent at worst. What you have instead is structure, commitment, and the accumulated evidence of having shown up for however many days you have completed. On the hard days, return to your contract. Return to your starting point page. Look at your habit tracker and count the days you have already completed. The motivation you are looking for is not a feeling, it is a record. Build the record every day, and return to it when you need reminding of who you are.

Can I do The 100 Method with someone else?

Yes, and for many people this significantly increases their likelihood of completing the 100 days. A shared commitment creates social accountability, the knowledge that someone else is on the same journey, facing the same challenges, showing up alongside you. If you choose to do this, the most important thing is that each person has their own goal. Not the same goal, their own. The method works because of singular focus. Two people can walk the same path with entirely different destinations.

You celebrate. You complete the final reflection in your planner, honestly and fully. You sit with what you have accomplished, not just the goal but the identity. And then, when you are ready, you begin again. The 100 Method is designed to be repeatable. Every goal worth pursuing can be a 100-day commitment. Every version of yourself worth becoming can be built one 100-day journey at a time. Day 100 is not the end. It is the proof that you can do it, and the beginning of everything that comes next.

"The question that matters most is not any of these. It is: will you begin?"

THE 100 METHOD
MANIFESTO

We believe that every person carries a goal worth pursuing.

We believe that the gap between where you are and where you want to be

is not a gap of talent. It is a gap of method.

We believe that 100 minutes of focused daily effort,

applied to one goal over 100 days,

is enough to change not just what you achieve, but who you are.

We believe in accountability, the honest, unflinching practice

of seeing yourself clearly and choosing to grow.

We believe in consistency, not perfection,

but the steady, daily act of showing up when it would be easier not to.

We believe in discipline, not as restriction,

but as the deepest form of freedom available to any person.

And we believe in self-love, the foundational conviction

that you are worth showing up for.

This is not about motivation.

This is not about perfection.

This is about the decision to begin, and the commitment to continue.

100 Minutes.

100 Days.

1 Goal.

THE 100 METHOD™

NOTES

NOTES

NOTES

ACKNOWLEDGMENTS

This book was written for the person who has a goal they haven't yet achieved. For the one who has started before and stopped. For the one who is ready, more ready than they know, to do something differently this time.

Every idea in these pages was shaped by the simple observation that the gap between where most people are and where they want to be is not a gap of talent, intelligence, or potential. It is a gap of method. Of structure. Of the daily, disciplined practice of showing up for the thing that matters most.

To every person who picks up this book and makes the decision to begin: thank you. You are the reason this method exists. And you are proof that transformation is not reserved for a special category of person. It is available to anyone willing to show up for 100 minutes, for 100 days, in pursuit of one goal.

Go do the work.

— The 100 Method

ABOUT THE 100 METHOD

The 100 Method is a framework for transformation built on a single, powerful idea: that 100 minutes of focused daily effort, applied to one goal over 100 days, is enough to change not just what you achieve, but who you are.

The 100 Method exists to close the gap between the life people are living and the life they know they are capable of. Not through complicated systems or unsustainable intensity, but through clarity, consistency, and the daily practice of keeping your word to yourself.

The 100 Method Planner is the daily companion to this book. It provides the structure, the daily pages, the milestone check-ins, the reflection prompts, and the 100-day habit tracker, that brings everything in these pages to life.

ALSO FROM THE 100 METHOD

The 100 Method Plan

theonehundredmethod.com